This Book Belongs to

_____

Name:

RHYMES OF THE TIMES BLACK NURSERY RHYMES

Written by Audrey Muhammad

Illustrated by Kofi Johnson

Published By
Get Fit To Live
Raleigh, NC

Copyright 2017-2018
All Rights Reserved

No part of this book may be reproduced in any form without prior permission of the copyright owner

DEDICATION

This book is dedicated to the Mothers and Fathers of civilization and my beautiful daughter, Hasana.

Special thanks to The One God, my little sister Broyny for her time and talent, my brother Vincent and my wonderful parents, Ernest and Eva Flowers, for their unconditional love and support. Thank You! I love you!

Pretty Little Black Girl

Pretty little Black girl,
Smart and brave,
You have pretty curls and natural waves.
Be proud of the pretty hair that God gave.
You're a pretty little Black girl, Smart and brave.
Love yourself and see it's true,
Everyone wants to be as pretty as you!
Be proud of the pretty skin that God gave.
You're a pretty little Black girl, Smart and brave.

BRIGHT LIGHT LEWIS!

Lewis Latimer was
very bright:
he developed many patents
for the electric light.
They gave Thomas Edison the
credit for helping us see,
but Lewis Latimer had
the real key.

James A. Healy

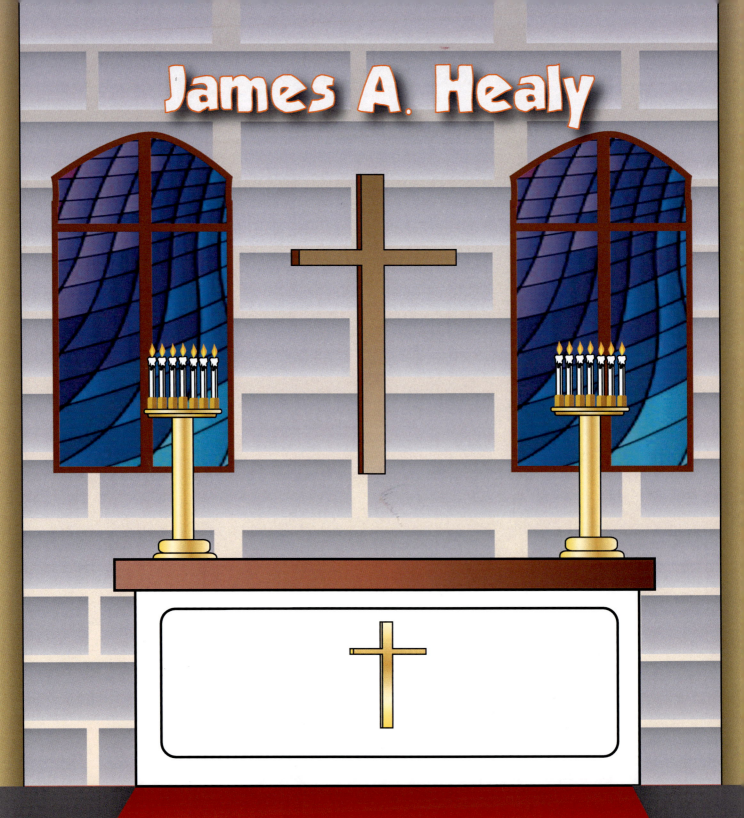

James A. Healy, the first Black Catholic Priest,
Was a holy Black man, to say the least.

He was appointed assistant to the Papal Throne
And did his best to uplift the Catholic dome.

Martin Had a Little Dream

Martin had a Little Dream, a little dream, a little dream.
Martin had a little dream of peace and equality.

But everywhere that Martin went, Martin went, Martin went;
Everywhere that Martin went he was treated unequally.

The dream followed him around the world, world one day, world one day
and he died before it came to be.

Sojourner Truth

Isabella Baumfree had a great vision.
Speaking the truth was her mission.

Sojourner Truth she then was called.
She wasn't afraid, not at all.

She worked tirelessly during the civil war.
A union win was what she fought for.

Sojourner Truth was a strong Black woman.
Remember her strength; remember her wisdom.

MOTHER AFRICA

"Motherland, Motherland,
Do you know who I am?"

Yes, you are my child.
Stolen from your homeland.

"Motherland, Motherland,
Can I come back?"

Yes, my child, hurry and pack.
But before you do, can I ask one thing?

"Yes, my mother,
My beautiful queen."

My child, my child,
Do you miss me much?

"Yes, my mother,
I long for your touch."

My child, my child, we must never separate again,
So beware of people who practice sins.

BOOKER T WASHINGTON

Booker T. Washington was a brilliant man.
He said we should use our minds, as well as our hands.

He taught Black people trades and how to read and write.
He believed in education and doing right.

He founded the Tuskegee Institute as a college.
He taught his people skills and much knowledge.

Booker T. Washington, a man for the people.
Booker T. Washington wanted us to be equals.

MALCOLM X

His nickname was Detroit Red.
He committed many crimes, in the early life he led.

Malcolm Little was his slave name,
When he was caught in the middle of society's game.

Malcolm became a strong Black leader.
Elijah Muhammad was his great teacher.

Elijah gave Malcolm an "X" in the place of his slave name.
From there, Malcolm ascended to fame.

He felt that Black people should do for self.
By any means necessary we should maintain our health;
And teach our children the knowledge of self.

Some say he was killed by the U.S. government for taking a stand
And reaching out to his fellow Black man.

Malcolm spoke out without much rest.
But remember, El-Hajj Malik El Shabazz was at his best
During the time he was Malcolm X.

GO GARRETT GO!

Go Garrett Go!
He made the stoplight
on the pole.

The red is to stop the killing.
The green is to go.
The yellow is for loving your people
And taking it slow.

Woman On The Bus

There was a young woman who sat on a bus.
She didn't talk much or cause much fuss.

One day she was asked to give up her seat,
Though she was quite tired and quite weak.

They wanted to put this Black woman down,
But Rosa Parks stood her ground.

She was arrested for refusing the bus driver's demand,
To give up her seat to a white man.

Rosa was a victim, we now understand,
Of unjust law in an unjust land.

The incident gave the Civil Rights movement a start.
It was the day Rosa Parks made her mark.

The Mandelas

South African Flag

Nelson and Winnie lived in a land of hate,
Where racist people refused to accept their fate.

30 million Blacks ruled by 4 million Whites.
Everybody knows that isn't right.

The Blacks couldn't vote or move freely around.
They were killed when they made the slightest sound.

Apartheid was the law that made racism legal.
Watch out racist ones, "Power to the People."

HUMBLE ELIJAH

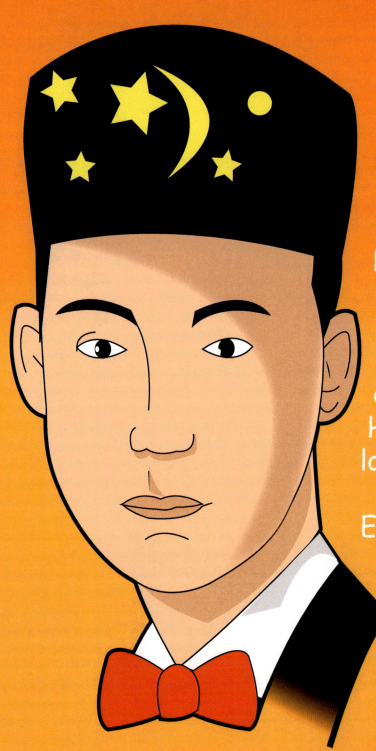

Elijah be humble,
Elijah be quick.
He is the leader we
should pick.

He taught us how to
eat to live.
He taught us how to
love Black and to give.

Elijah be humble,
Elijah be quick.
He is the leader we
should pick.

MORGAN'S GAS MASK!

Load them up, load them up,
My good brother man.

Get me out of the fumes
As fast as you can.

Give me the gas mask
Garrett Morgan made;

For it will save my life
When the enemy invades.

The Underground Railroad

The underground railroad wasn't a railroad at all.
It helped to free Black slaves and get them far.

It was a network and a hiding place,
Hiding Blacks from the slavemaster's face.

It helped Blacks escape from the
South to the North.
And many Blacks fought to come forth.

The railroad always stayed on track,
Rarely losing a passenger, and that's a fact!

Devoted Doctor Drew

Charles Drew sat in a car.
He had an accident and a great fall.

All the racist doctors and all the racist men
Wouldn't put Dr. Drew back together again.

Treatment was refused to this brilliant Black man
Because their hospitals did not allow "negroes" in.

Dr. Drew's life, however, was not in vain.
His work with blood banks and plasma helped to heal much pain.

FREDERICK DOUGLASS

Mr. Douglass founded the North Star Newspaper
And wrote about the evils of all the slavemasters.

He said Black men have to fight
To end the slavemaster's wicked plight.

Brave Black men fought in the civil war.
They would rather die free than be slaves anymore.

After the war, Douglass continued to speak out.
Taking care of business was what he was about.

He wanted Blacks to have an education, land, and civil rights.
He said Black men must continue their fight.

Douglass fought against an unjust law and an unjust nation.
He wanted to keep Blacks off the plantation.

THIS YOUNG BLACK MALE

This young Black male could play ball.
This young Black male could not.
This young Black male went to the mall.
This young Black male studied a lot.
He went to college and gained lots of knowledge,
Then returned home to reclaim his throne.

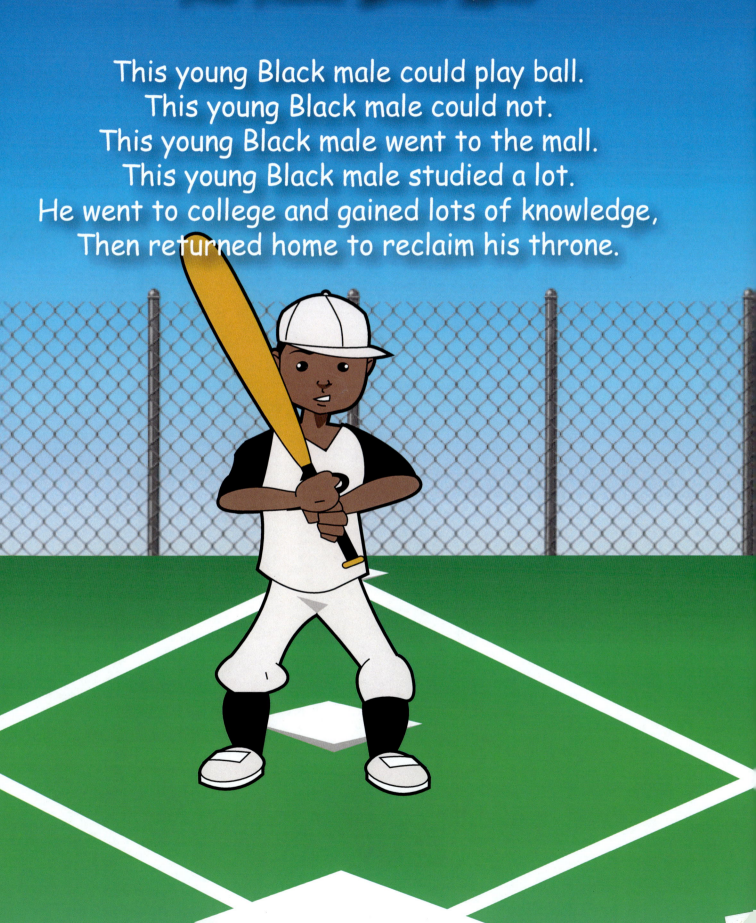

OPRAH OPRAH

Oprah, Oprah,
First Black Female Billionaire
She has style, class, and gorgeous hair.

Oprah, Oprah,
Has a brilliant mind and is ahead of her time,
She has her OWN network and nursery rhyme!

Oprah, Oprah,
A Media guru,
If she can do it,
You can too!

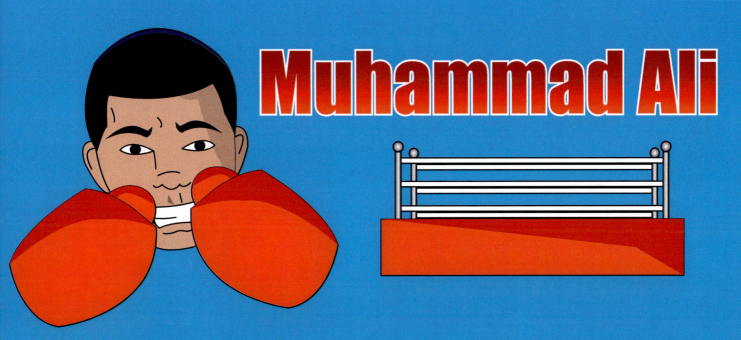

Muhammad Ali

Muhammad Ali, the best boxer in the ring.
"I am the Greatest," he would sing!

He could "float like a butterfly and sting like a bee,"
everyone knows his name, Muhammad Ali.

He stood on principle and spoke the truth.
He was an inspiration to many world youth.

He could "float like a butterfly and sting like a bee,"
everyone knows his name, Muhammad Ali.

He was a champion of freedom and a teacher of peace.
He always tried to help the poor and the least.

He could "float like a butterfly and sting like a bee,"
everyone knows his name, Muhammad Ali.

Off to the White House

Yes, he can, Yes he can!
Off to the White House
A very wise man.

The First Black President
To walk through the door
Along with Michelle, Malia, and Sasha,
He's number 44!

A lawyer by trade
A man well-made.
Yes, he can, yes he can,
Off to the White House
A very wise man.

He united the people
And the country too,
Yes, he did, and we can too!

Yes, we can, yes we can,
Off to the White House,
A very wise man.

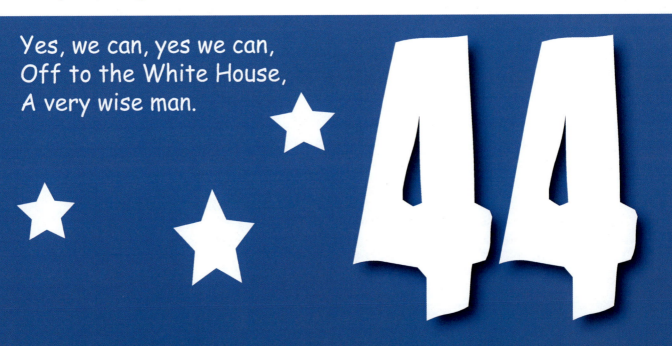

THINK LIKE STEVE

Think like Steve
And write good jokes.

Think like Steve
And give youth Hope.

Think like Steve
And chart your success;
Write good books
And do your best.

Think like Steve
And host Family Feud.
Be like Steve Harvey,
He is one cool dude.

"Walk by Faith And Master Your Mind"

Walk by faith and Master your mind,
Joe L. Dudley is one of a kind.

He grew up in a poor family in the South,
His family barely had food for their mouths.

He had a vision and a determination to sell
So he went door-to-door in direct sales.

He invested $10 in his first sales kit.
Soon, his hair care products were a big hit!

S.B. Fuller was his mentor and friend
Their Mastermind Groups inspired a trend.

Walk by faith and Master your mind,
Joe L. Dudley is one of a kind.

Made in the USA
Columbia, SC
06 July 2021